HER NAME IS

Wisdom

WISDOM'S TRUE IDENTITY IS REVEALED

WILLIE FAULKNER

HER NAME IS

Wisdom

WISDOM'S TRUE IDENTITY IS REVEALED

ISBN: 979-8-9911307-0-7

Printed in the United States of America

For permissions requests, please contact:
ELEAT Publishing, LLC
www.eleatpublishing.com
info@eleatpublishing.com

HER NAME IS

Wisdom

WISDOM'S TRUE IDENTITY IS REVEALED

Table of Contents

INTRODUCTION

CHAPTER ONE:
WHAT IS WISDOM?   **1**
    Zipporah is Given Wisdom   8

CHAPTER TWO:
WISDOM'S MEANING   **14**

CHAPTER THREE:
WISDOM'S PURPOSE   **21**
    Wisdom: Skill in Living   21
    Wisdom at Jericho   24
    Wisdom: Operating in Lives   27
    Rahab finds Wisdom   28

CHAPTER FOUR:
THREE SOURCES OF WISDOM   **33**
    Godly Wisdom   34
    The When of Wisdom   38
    The Forgotten Poor Wise Man   39
    Man's Worldly Wisdom   40
    Satan's Wisdom   45

CHAPTER FIVE:
LADY WISDOM   **49**
    Is The Holy Spirit a He?   55
    Lady Wisdom in the New Testament   56
    Jesus calls Wisdom "Her"   58

ABOUT THE AUTHOR   **60**

INTRODUCTION

Get wisdom, get understanding: forget it not; neither decline from the words of my mouth. Forsake her not, and she shall preserve thee: love her, and she shall keep thee. Wisdom is the principal thing; therefore get wisdom: and with all thy getting, get understanding. Exalt her, and she shall promote thee: she shall bring thee to honor, when thou dost embrace her. She shall give to thine head an ornament of grace, a crown of glory shall she deliver to thee. (Proverbs 4:5-9).

The voice that is crying and speaking is Wisdom. And it is time to properly introduce you to her. That is right, "her." Wisdom which has been sought after, preached and taught; studied, envied, dissected and proclaimed. The rich and the poor have desired wisdom. The strong and the weak want to possess wisdom. Both the simple and famous hunger for her. The simple and brilliant minded thirst for wisdom's words. Men and Women used her throughout the centuries but she is still full. Never lacking, never ending, never prejudice or bias; wisdom was, is and will always be available to all those who ask for her.

The question is why has there has not been a man or woman throughout history or the present day, who has dared to ask or state the obvious concerning one of the most important spiritual words'; virtues'; gifts'; or persons', in the Bible! Why is wisdom called "her"? Why is wisdom referred to as "she"? Why have both men and women, brothers and sisters, mothers and fathers, boys and girls, priests and nuns, saints and sinners, Jews and Gentiles, church leaders and members refused to consider that in the male dominated theme of the Bible that one of the most important keys of the Bible is a female? Even though the Bible plainly tells us that wisdom is not a male, but a female. A female "what" you might ask? Blasphemy, some would say!

Most Christians believe that Wisdom is the Holy Spirit, or Jesus, or God, or a gift. And the use of "her" or "she" can be explained by the poetic nature of the chapters in the Book of Proverbs. So, what about you? Today, you will be challenged to think for yourself. That is what makes reading so liberating. I know what you have been told and what you heard; because all my life I was in the same school of learning, until Wisdom spoke to me. This is what she said.

CHAPTER ONE:
WHAT IS WISDOM?

Wisdom is like a free-flowing river providing life to all who partake of it. In some places wisdom is shallow but in other places it overflows. Wisdom can also be described as a well whose source is deep and unseen and can be found in the most barren of places. When I think of wisdom, it is in terms of the ocean. Its borders are invisible and depths are unsearchable. Like an ocean, wisdom gives and sustains life. For those who possess wisdom a storm can rage on the outside, while there is order and peace on the inside. These are all examples of what wisdom can be compared to in the *natural world*, but it would be useful to answer the following: What is wisdom in its *biblical* context?

To answer this question, we will turn to a surprising scripture in the Bible. What's surprising is that this scripture is not found in the book that you would expect to find it in, which is the book of Proverbs. When you think of the word *wisdom*, Proverbs naturally comes to mind because it mentions wisdom thirty-one times, and that is more than any other book in the Bible. Although Solomon was the wisest man that ever lived (except for Jesus) and the author of Proverbs, there are several unidentified wise men who are credited with writing several of the chapters—Agur and Lemuel.

The book of Exodus, written by Moses, contains a revealing look into the identity of wisdom. Hidden in Chapter 28 is a gem of a verse that has been hidden in plain sight, just waiting to be uncovered:

> *Exodus 28:3, "and thou shalt speak unto all that are wise hearted, whom I have filled with the spirit of wisdom, that they may make Aaron's garments to consecrate him, that he may minister unto me in the priest's office."*

There are some questions which needs to be addressed in the text that will help us see what wisdom is:

1. Did God fill some of the men of the children of Israel with the spirit of wisdom thus leading them to be looked upon by the people as wise hearted?

By simply pulling from what the text is saying we can get some clear facts about wisdom. God can give wisdom to whomever he desires without them asking for it. This is not in contradiction to James 1:5, which says that "if any of you lack wisdom, let him ask of God, that giveth to all men liberally, and upbraided not; and it shall be given him." To the contrary, it reflects what James is saying and adds the dynamic that in addition to God giving wisdom liberally to any man whether a believer or unbeliever: if a person asks for it, God hears them and will grant their request if He decides to.

Looking back at the text, in Exodus, we notice a very important truth confirmed by scripture: God, in fact, gave the people a spirit of wisdom.

2. Did God fill them with the knowledge and skill to design and make garments for the priests that they did not possess?

The text from Exodus informs us that God gives mankind the skill and knowledge to work, live, create, invent and imagine all things through wisdom. The Book of Exodus is full of examples of the children of Israel using wisdom to build and create things pertaining to the temple. The skill and workmanship attained is undoubtedly a result of divine instruction causing the children of Israel to excel. In short, God imparts wisdom which 1) enhances a person's own knowledge and abilities or

2) imparts knowledge and abilities to a person who doesn't possess it. And he will do the same thing for us today.

We are challenged by the word of God that if we need wisdom in our lives no matter what the situation, God is anxiously waiting for us to ask him for his wisdom. James, the brother of Jesus, in his Epistle to the early church includes a scripture which best reflects God's desire to share spiritual gifts with his creation.

> *James 1:7, "If any of you lack wisdom, let him ask of God, that giveth to all men liberally, and upbraideth not, and it shall be given him."*

So, what is wisdom? Wisdom is not God or God the Father. This still leaves open the possibility that wisdom as most believe, can be Jesus/ The Lord, The Holy Spirit.

Perhaps the most famous account recorded in the Bible concerning Wisdom centers around King Solomon receiving wisdom from God after asking for it in a dream. Then King Solomon is faced with an unbelievable court case. A mother claims that another woman replaced her baby which is alive with a dead baby. The case was so complex that no one could discern who was lying and who was telling the truth. King Solomon ordered for his servant to bring a sword and he proceeded to cut the child in half and said that he would give half to each mother; but the real mother cried out and said the child should be given to the other woman.

King Solomon rendered his verdict by decreeing and giving the baby to the woman who cried out who he declared was the baby's real mother. 1 Kings 3:28, records the reaction of people when witnessing Godly wisdom on display. "And all Israel heard of the judgment which the king had judged; and they feared the king, for they saw that the wisdom of God was in him, to do judgment."

With that being said, there can be no doubt that Wisdom is a Spirit. Not convinced? Let's flip the pages of the Bible to its last book, Revelation.

> *Revelation 1:4, "John to the seven churches which are in Asia: Grace be unto you, and peace, from him which is, and*

3

> *was, and which is to come; and from the seven Spirits which are before his throne."*

"Revelation," in the Greek translation, means "apokalypsis" or the unveiling of something previously unrevealed. The Holy Spirit shows Paul the mysteries concerning Christ and his eternal plan. Ironically the last book of the Bible is where we begin a provocative truth relating to the identity of Wisdom.

There are seven Spirits before the throne of God, and it is important that we know who or what these seven spirits are. And let's keep in mind that we are hoping to find the name of one spirit in particular— Wisdom. Revelation 1:4 leads us to Revelation 4:5, another scripture relating to the seven Spirits.

> *Revelation 4:5, "and out of the throne proceeded lightnings and thunderings and voices: and there were seven lamps of fire burning before the throne, which are the seven Spirits of God."*

Again, the text reveals or confirms the presence of the seven Spirits. These are seven distinct or different Spirits ordained or set aside by God. Revelations 5:6 is the third and final scripture mentioning the seven spirits. "And I beheld, and, lo, in the midst of the throne and of the four beasts, and in the midst of the elders stood a Lamb as if it had been slain, having seven horns and seven eyes, which are the seven spirits of God sent forth into all the earth."

This verse reveals a mystery that has been overlooked or gone unnoticed until now. Buried for centuries is an astonishing truth which will change the way we see Jesus, the seven spirits, and wisdom. It's obvious that the Lamb is the Lion of the tribe of Judah, the Root of David, who we call Jesus. The Lamb has in his possession seven horns and seven eyes which are the seven spirits of God. The Lamb is not the one being sent forth into all the earth; but, the seven spirits are the ones sent. This simple truth proves that Jesus isn't the seven spirits of God; but the Son of God!

The meaning of the verse centers on the word "having". Having, or to have is defined as; to hold in one's use, service, regard. And to hold in one's possession. Jesus is seen as the Lamb and not the seven spirits of God. He is the Son of God and the third part of the trinity. The text clearly testifies that the Lamb is holding or in possession of the seven spirits for his use and service as depicted by them being sent forth into all the world. Finally, the seven spirits are plural and Jesus, The Lamb, the Lion of the Tribe of Judah is singular.

But there are no names associated with these seven Spirits; and that is a problem. To solve this problem, we must turn our attention to an Old Testament prophet—one who holds the title of being called, the eagle eye prophet, Isaiah.

> *Isaiah 11:1-2, "and there shall come forth a rod out of the stem of Jesse, and a branch shall grow out of his roots. And the spirit of the Lord shall rest upon him, the spirit of wisdom and, the spirit of understanding, the spirit of counsel, and the spirit of might, and the spirit of knowledge, and the spirit of the fear of the Lord."*

The first part of this scripture focuses on the Messiah. The Messiah will be a direct Descendant of Jesse who is the father of King David. Jesus meets the criteria through Joseph and Mary. Isaiah testifies that the Messiah shall possess the seven spirits mentioned.

The Jewish "menora" or candlestick best illustrates its positioning and likeness. Found in Exodus 25:31-40, the Menorah, made of seven branches and a base with only the middle branch, the longest part is connected to the base. This middle branch is straight and reaches up to eternity. The middle branch is named, The Spirit of the Lord. There are six branches attached to the center branch of the Menorah.

Three branches on the right side and three branches on the left. Each branch is positioned directly across from the other while being tiered under each other. These six branches extend out from the center branch and reach upward toward eternity like the center branch. The six branches are named: Spirit of Wisdom, Spirit of Understanding, Spirit of Counsel, Spirit of Might, Spirit of Knowledge, and Spirit of the fear of the Lord. Isaiah is testifying that only the Messiah will possess all of these Seven Spirits at one time.

Hidden in plain sight is a list of the Seven Spirits:

1. Spirit of the Lord
2. Spirit of Wisdom
3. Spirit of Understanding
4. Spirit of Counsel
5. Spirit of Might
6. Spirit of Knowledge
7. Spirit of the Fear of the Lord

The idea that the Holy Spirit, Wisdom and the Seven Spirits mentioned in Revelation are one being is a theory. The idea that the Holy Spirit is wisdom via the seven spirits of God mentioned in Revelation ignores Galatians 5:22-23, "But the fruit of the Spirit is love, joy, peace, long suffering, gentleness, goodness, faith, meekness and temperance." Additionally Ephesians 1:13-17, reveals another hidden fact concerning the Holy Spirit and Wisdom. Verses thirteen and fourteen explain the gospel which includes Christians or believers being filled or sealed with the Holy Spirit. Afterwards, we are led by the text to the seventeenth verse which clearly testifies that God will give to these same Christians and believers who have already received the Holy Spirit—the Spirit of Wisdom. This proves one thing: the Holy Spirit and the Spirit of Wisdom are not the same.

Without a doubt, the evidence is solid. Wisdom *is* a spirit. And it is one of the seven spirits. Now that we know what Wisdom *is*, let's look at what Wisdom is *not*.

1. Wisdom is not a gift
2. Wisdom is not The Holy Spirit
3. Wisdom is not Jesus / The Lord.

It is important to note that the text in Exodus demonstrates why God can't be Wisdom for another reason. God can't give wisdom *and* be wisdom at the same time.

To help us further understand wisdom and its purpose, there are three objectives in the scriptures that need to be addressed along with some other perspectives which will be highlighted.

1. Wisdom is given to mankind to make known to us the higher perspective by which God understands things and what God expects and requires of us that we are incapable of understanding without the Spirit of Wisdom.

2. A Christian or Believer with the inspiration of the Spirit of Wisdom should have a true understanding concerning life which a Non-Christian or Non-Believer does not possess.

3. Wisdom—which at times symbolizes Jesus Christ as mentioned in 1 Corinthians 1:24—should be operating in the lives of Christians.

   1 Corinthians 1:24: "But unto them which are called, both Jews and Greeks, Christ the power of God, and the wisdom of God"

Again, this is not contradicting what has been previously brought to light about wisdom. Remember in scripture, Jesus is identified by many adjectives such as, the bread of life, stone that the builders rejected, seed of a woman, bright and morning star, etc. Noticeably, Jesus is the only person in history that possesses all the fullness of the Godhead in physical form. Simply put, during His time on earth Jesus was not only equipped with all power and spiritual attributes, but he was a master of their purposes.

Zipporah is Given Wisdom

This chapter is going to end with a story in the Bible that is often overlooked. And one of the reasons why is because the main person is a woman. With that being said, perhaps the best way to begin the story and end the chapter is with a question: What happens when the deliverer needs deliverance?

When we think of a deliverer in the Bible the most famous person can be found in the Old Testament or Old Covenant because the word *testament* means "covenant." One of the most pivotal events in scripture could have been altered if not for the cunning of a very wise woman named Zipporah who was Moses' first wife. Her being identified as the first wife is relevant due to the omission of Moses being married twice. No one likes to talk about it for a couple of reasons. One being that either Zipporah died or he got a divorce from her. The second and most important has to do with his second wife being an Ethiopian or a Cushite woman. This can be found by referencing Numbers 12:1, "And Miriam and Aaron spoke against Moses because of the Ethiopian woman whom he had married; for he had married an Ethiopian woman."

It is entirely possible that Aaron or Joshua could have delivered the children of Israel from Egypt if not for this overlooked passage of scripture mentioned in the book of Exodus. After Moses encountered the Burning Bush and received the Rod. After Aaron was appointed the mouthpiece for Moses because of his reluctance to do so; and just before Moses began his return to Egypt to deliver Gods' children accompanied by his wife and two sons; Gershom – the first born, and Eliezer. History begins to record this earth-shattering event unfolding right before our very eyes.

But before we dive into this overlooked passage of scripture there are two other scriptures that will help us understand our subject scripture. In the book of Genesis the seventeenth chapter and the thirteenth and fourteenth verses we find that part of the covenant God made with Abraham concerning his seed, especially all males born in a house. Circumcision in God's eyes represented dedication to God and was a main ingredient to the covenant. Unknown to most believers today is the fact that circumcision of males was not unique to Abraham and Israel during this time period. For the Israelites, circumcision itself serves as an outward sign of inward dedication to God. Let's take a look at our scripture of focus:

> *Genesis 17:13-14, "he that is born in thy house, and he that is bought with thy money, must needs be circumcised: and my covenant shall be in your flesh for an everlasting covenant. And the uncircumcised man child whose flesh of his foreskin is not circumcised, that soul shall be cut off from his people; he hath broken my covenant."*

What precedes these verses is God instructing Moses that he is to perform signs, wonders and miracles before Pharaoh with the rod that he carries; but Pharaoh's heart will be hardened, and he will not let the children of Israel go. This leads us directly to Exodus 4: 22-23. Just like the other scriptures these two carry hidden ingredients that will help us understand the subject scripture that we are about to dive into. For instance the Nation of Israel living in Egypt in God's view is His Son; God's first born, Son. Egypt is enslaving God's child: not children, but child singular and God is their Father. Drawing from the scripture we can see the relationship God has with the Nation of Israel.

Israel is God's first- born child. Which means that all mankind or nations are his children. However, Israel holds the distinction of being His firstborn child. They are not better or loved more by God, but their place as being the first born holds a special place in the family. This my brothers and sisters is why Moses is instructed by God to tell Pharaoh to let His Child or Son go, and the consequences of not letting Israel go is that Egypt's firstborn son will be cut off or killed. This is an astonishing revelation hidden in the text. Now we can understand and stop questioning why the first-born males of Egypt were cut off or killed.

> *Exodus 4:22-23, "And thou shalt say unto Pharaoh, thus sayeth the Lord, Israel is my son, even my first- born: And I say unto thee, let my son go, that he may serve me: and if thou refuse to let him go, behold I will slay thou son, even thou first-born."*

So, the punishment for Egypt enslaving, punishing, killing and not freeing Israel, God's first- born son, is a sentence against Egypt's first-born son.

9

Exodus 4:24-26, "and it came to pass by the way in the inn, that the Lord met him, and sought to kill him. Then Zipporah took a sharp stone, and cut off the foreskin of her son, and cast it at his feet, and said, Surely a bloody husband art thou to me. So, he let him go then she said, A bloody husband thou art, because of the circumcision."

Moses along with his wife and their two sons are preparing to head back to Egypt as directed by God. Right before leaving God tells Moses that Aaron has left Egypt and is on his way through the wilderness to meet up with them which takes place in the twenty-seventh verse. In taking a closer look at the text we **can** see another truth which has been hidden or overlooked. The scripture reveals that the family left their home and the mountain of God and headed on a trip towards Egypt with the purpose of delivering Israel from slavery in Egypt through the power and guidance of the God of Israel.

The text highlights a major common sense truth that existed. In the twenty-fourth verse the bible says that the Lord met them on the way after they left or passed by the inn. This text has been screaming out for centuries to be heard. Could this be the same inn that Joseph's brothers stopped on their way to and from Egypt during the famine. In fact, Genesis 42:27, clearly states that one of Joseph's brothers opened his sack in the inn and found that his money had been restored to him. The money that they had paid Joseph their brother: whom they sold into bondage, for food and supplies, was secretly given back to them by Joseph, who they didn't recognize and who was given an Egyptian name. Joseph secretly set his brothers up to prove or test them. Ironically, God does the same thing to us at times by allowing circumstances to enter into our lives.

That's enough of a detour, let's get back to this hidden truth. We have been led to believe that when Moses left Egypt he wandered through the desert and wilderness without any food or water and by chance came upon Jethro's home. Jethro was a priest of Midian. Midian lived in a region between Sinai and Arabia. The Bible clearly suggests what historians and archeologists have known for centuries: Egypt was the Rome of its day and all roads led to Egypt. There were major trade routes and roads leading into Egypt from all of Asia and Africa. These verses confirm there were inns and ways or roads both into and out of Egypt. Furthermore, this explains how they were able to meet Aaron on their way to Egypt, who was on his way to Median from Egypt to meet Moses due to the leading of God.

With the foundation being laid it is time to dive into our over-look passage of scripture, which will answer the question posed earlier; and that is, what happens when the deliverer needs deliverance. The deliverer being Moses of course and the person who delivers him is found in Exodus 4:24 through 26, "And it came to pass by the way in the inn, that the Lord met him, and sought to kill him. Then Zipporah took a sharp stone, and cut off the foreskin of her son, and cast it at his feet, and said, Surely a bloody husband art thou to me. So, he let him go, then she said, "A bloody husband thou art, because of the circumcision."

Drawing from what the text is saying and what we have learned thus far, it is plain to see that Moses and his family stopped at an inn which was located on a major route or road leading to Egypt. While there, God met him and is about to do the unthinkable, which is to kill Moses and his first-born son. But why is this incident not discussed, taught or preached about in religious circles? I hope it is not because of the hero in the story. The deliverer who delivered Moses from certain death. That person's name is Zipporah, the wife of Moses. However, there is another question that needs addressing before we move on; why would the Lord want to kill Moses and his son?

Moses was born a Hebrew or Israelite but because of Pharaoh's decree to kill all the Hebrew Males born in the land of Egypt. His mother placed him in a basket and floated him down the Nile River where Pharoah's sister's maidens found him. Although he was born a Hebrew, Moses was raised in Pharaoh's household as an Egyptian and Pharoah's nephew. Ironically, it was Moses's own Hebrew mother who was selected to raise him as a servant for Pharoah's sister. What a blessing. The Lord arranged for his mother to raise him and get paid doing so. However, due to the fact that the Egyptians did not believe in circumcisions and Moses was being raised as an Egyptian in Pharaoh's household; he was never circumcised.

Adding to the problem, was the fact that Moses did not circumcise his two sons. This was a direct violation of God's Covenant with his people, besides God had already given him a hint in the twenty-second and third verses concerning the pending doom of the Egyptians' first-born male children which is a direct reflection based on the Covenant with Abraham and his seed; Israel. Still, why would The Lord kill Moses and his first-born son, is the question?

The answer is in plain sight. Somehow, someway Zipporah knew what was going on and why. Instinctively she went into action and searched for a sharp object while realizing that The Lord required sacrifice. Moses was openly violating God's Covenant by ignoring the circumcision and was not even aware of it, but his wife was. She had the wisdom, knowledge and courage to circumcise her son and then Moses; and the only way she could have known was that Moses taught her about The Covenant of Abraham and its importance. This means that Moses knew. And that is why The Lord sought to kill him. Seeing what God was about to do, Zipporah, a wise woman, saved both her husband and son with a sharp stone. A stone that is sharper than any two-edged sword which represents the Word of God. In short, she used The Word to fulfill God's Covenant.

This wise woman, named Zipporah, needs to be celebrated for delivering the deliverer. By asking questions of the text we see that the story takes place while they were at the inn, before arriving or after leaving the inn. One thing we can be certain of is that The Lord met them with the purpose of taking the lives of Moses and his first-born son for breaking the Covenant. Most likely there must have been physical signs that Moses and his son's life were in peril; and, undoubtedly the source was coming from the presence of The Lord. Furthermore, there is no doubt that Zipporah knew that a debt was owed and had to be paid at that very moment. Realizing what needed to be done she cut off the foreskin of her first-born son and threw it at his feet; and said a bloody husband art thou to me. Then for her final act, Zipporah turned to Moses and cut off his foreskin and threw it at his feet and repeated the same words; a bloody husband art thou to me.

By not only reading the text and drawing from the text but asking questions of it, we find an amazing discovery. This was a precursor to the Passover, in fact it was a Passover, because when The Lord saw the blood, death passed over both Moses and his first-born son. Before the Passover had ever happened, which is celebrated today, we have this historical record of another Passover that predated the Egyptian account. Moses the deliverer was delivered from death due to the blood. What a blessing and a revelation hidden in plain sight. Surely this personal encounter with The Lord would only serve to expand their faith in the Covenant, The Word of God, and the Lord. Zipporah made sure that we would not overlook this event because she mentioned the blood twice, to let us know that she performed two circumcisions. And, that we would not miss the importance of The Blood and God's Covenant. Zipporah threw the bloody skin at Moses's feet twice and made mention of the blood each time so that death would Passover them both. Clearly Zipporah knew that her actions or sacrifice would satisfy The Lord's requirements.

With Moses being the author of the Book of Exodus a person would think that his wife Zipporah who saved his son's life and his; would be mentioned more often, however, her name is never mentioned again. There can only be a few reasons why she is never spoken of again: either she left Moses, she died, they divorced or Moses had two wives when he married the Ethiopian Woman. No matter what the case, one thing we can be sure of; Zipporah delivered her first-born son and Moses (The Deliverer) from death.

CHAPTER TWO:
WISDOM'S MEANING

Whether we are using wisdom for earthly reasons or spiritual ones, there seems to be a common belief that wisdom's definition looks like this: wisdom is laws and principles applied correctly; or wisdom is applying knowledge (information) and understanding (comprehension) correctly. Both groups have in essence created a formula for the word we call wisdom which looks like this:

Wisdom = applying laws and principles correctly.

Wisdom = applying knowledge and understanding correctly.

Wisdom = applying information and comprehension correctly.

This sounds simple enough and easy to follow, however, in the first example, a person must first have knowledge of laws and principles in order to use or apply wisdom. The same is true in the second and third examples: a person must have knowledge and understanding or information and comprehension in order to use or apply wisdom. This rational or explanation dealing with the definition of wisdom doesn't line up with what we have uncovered thus far from the Bible.

We have discovered from The Bible that wisdom is a spirit. The Hebrews or Israel who left Egypt after years of bondage were given wisdom by God which enabled them to become skillful craftsmen in designing and making the Priest Garments, The Tabernacle and all of its Furnishings and Vessels.

They had no way of knowing or understanding what they were doing because The Priests Garments, The Tabernacle and all the Holy Furnishings and Vessels were a pattern of things in Heaven. And there is Zipporah; how did she know that The Lord required a blood sacrifice or circumcision when apparently Moses didn't even know? Then, what are we going to do with this well-known scripture?

> *James 1:5, "if any of you lack wisdom, let him ask of God, that giveth to all men liberally, and upbraided not; and it shall be given him."*

This text clearly expresses that anyone can have wisdom regardless of whether they possess the knowledge of laws, principles, understanding, information, comprehension and/or knowledge itself, because God will give wisdom to any person who asks for it liberally and freely. Hence having any of the above is clearly not a requirement to having or using wisdom. The intent here is not to discredit or undermine the previous well known and established definition/application for the word we call wisdom; but by adding on to what is already known, hopefully a more accurate and detailed picture of the meaning of the word will come into view.

Let's begin to go into the dark room and develop a clear picture of the word wisdom so we can see it in all its glory or purpose, resulting in a more fulfilling common sense or practical definition/application for its use. For the sake of time there is one story in the Bible that we are going to glean from.

> *Matthew 16:13-17, "when Jesus came into the coasts of Caesarea Philippi, he asked his disciples, saying, "Whom do men say that I, the Son of Man am? And they said, some say that thou art John the Baptist: some Elijah; and others, Jeremiah, or one of the prophets. He saith unto them, but whom say ye that I am? And Simon Peter answered and said, Thou art The Christ, the Son of The Living God. And Jesus answered and said unto him, Blessed art thou Simon Bar-jona:*

for flesh and blood have not revealed it unto thee, but my Father which is in Heaven."

One thing that I love to do when reading the Bible is to put myself in that moment when what I am reading on the page is taking place. Jesus and his disciples had just left Bethsaida where a blind man was healed and received his sight. At first, after Jesus healed him, the blind man saw men as trees, meaning that his vision wasn't quite right. The blind man was able to see people clearly or the way they looked once Jesus added to the healing process by putting his hands upon him the second time. Likewise, this is the result that we are looking for in our study of wisdom. The desire is that the person attempting to be wise or apply wisdom will be more successful because they can understand the meaning of wisdom more clearly, resulting in a more favorable outcome when used. Jesus and the disciples are coming upon Caesarea Philippi, a town northeast of Galilee, near the Jordan River. For some strange reason Jesus ask them an off the wall question: one that comes right out of left field.

A question that was probably not expected because it had nothing to do with what just happened with the blind man or what they might encounter in Caesarea. Instead, Jesus asks his disciples, "Who do people say that I am?" In other words, what is the latest gossip about me? Who do I act like? Who do I pray like? Who do I preach like? Who do I heal like? Who do they think I am? Because they are not going to ask me; they are going to ask you because you are close to me. I am asking you guys because I am close to you.

What a question. Jesus, the most popular and mysterious person in all of Israel and the Roman Empire, is asking a question that doesn't have anything to do with a right or wrong answer. A question having nothing to do with faith. A question having nothing to do with a parable.

Without hesitation the disciples began answering because they felt comfortable. They were being asked to do something that they had done all their lives and were probably doing behind Jesus's back, gossiping. The disciples were in their comfort zone. They didn't have to worry about watching what they were saying because they were not hurting anyone or anything. For that brief unexpected moment it was like Jesus was one of the boys. But then the master turned a three-sixty on them. While the disciples were feeling relaxed and at ease. Jesus grabbed the question out of mid- air and put the question right in their face. Hey guys, who do you think I am? Suddenly the atmosphere changed and the disciples' facial countenance changed due to the strategic positioning of the question. The question is now personal and there is an unexpected silence. The disciples didn't know what to say. Looking at each other with stoned faces, some were probably thinking, he did it again!

While the disciples were thinking of something suitable to say, the silence was interrupted by Peters' loud and victorious voice proclaiming statements that shocked even him; "thou art The Christ, The Son of The Living God!"

Jesus informs Peter, the disciples and all future readers of the text that flesh and blood did not reveal unto him the truth that he just stated. Nobody on earth knew that Jesus was the Messiah. The disciples were hoping that Jesus was the Messiah, but they were expecting a natural deliverer resembling that of Moses. They were hoping for a kingdom on earth with Jesus being the king with them expecting to receive positions in the new kingdom once Jesus overthrew the Roman Empire.

However, nobody thought that Jesus was God's Son or The Son of God, not even his disciples or Peter. In fact, they considered such a statement as blasphemy and worthy of death. Jesus makes it clear that Peter's confession was true; but the source did not come from Peter's own knowledge, information, comprehension, understanding or principles that he may have learned or considered from any outside source. This includes by means of studying from or listening to other people's perspectives on the subject.

The fact of the matter is that God, or Jesus Father, who is in heaven; revealed this wisdom to Peter. Let's make it clear, Peter had no prior knowledge of the wisdom which came out of his mouth. There can be no denying the fact that the wise statement proclaimed by Peter was given to him by the Spirit of God, because Jesus himself declares it. This is further evidence that wisdom can be divinely given. Before digging deeper, it is a good time to pause and introduce a complete definition and formula concerning wisdom:

Wisdom =

- applying laws and principles correctly through (revelation, gift, inspiration, discernment)

- applying knowledge and understanding through (revelation, gift, inspiration, discernment)

- applying information and comprehension through (revelation, gift, inspiration, discernment)

The difference between this new concept and the old is two-fold. The old meaning dealing with wisdom requires a person to have the knowledge of something in order to be wise in that area. Secondly, it suggests that a person can't be wise without possessing something that relates to the wisdom being portrayed. But the new meaning adds another dimension to the equation. A person doesn't have to have any prior knowledge of something in order to be wise in an area, because their wisdom is spiritually revealed. And a person's knowledge of something can be multiplied through inspiration of the spirit resulting in wisdom's birth.

The essence of wisdom or Godly Wisdom is that it leads to an eternal purpose or view of a thing. A view that holds true throughout eternity, or from generation to generation. This type of wisdom is related to old clichés like mother wit. Mother Wit is a type of wisdom dealing with a mother's wisdom. A mother who in my mother's and grandmother's days, was likely uneducated but taught her children, the neighbor's children and in many instances her employers or slave masters' children the facts of life; the meaning of life, and the purpose of life. Somehow and some way, they knew not only what to do but how to do it.

For instance my grandmother did not know how to read or write. However, she could look at a dress or suit and without seeing or studying the pattern, she could sew and create that exact dress or suit just by looking at it. In fact, she made all her dresses and she always dressed sharp. Just think of how much money she saved her family and how much money she made for her family.

Then, there is common sense which isn't so common anymore. One reason being we are not asking God for wisdom but we are looking for men and women who have a title, a position, or a name associated with them. Hence, we are getting what Jesus told Peter. Flesh and blood can reveal things to us, but it doesn't measure up to God's. There is no doubting the fact that a person can have the gift of wisdom. And with wisdom being a spirit it makes sense that wisdom can come by means of revelation, inspiration, discernment and impartation. All of these can be found in the Biblical Stories and are applicable in understanding the presence of wisdom operating in a person's life.

Honestly, how many people have surprised us with the wisdom being demonstrated in their lives? A good example is the life of Martin Luther King, Jr. Many people forget how young Dr. King was when he was thrust into the national spotlight as the leader of the Civil Rights Movement. He was in his late twenties, yet he possessed the wisdom of a much older man. Unlike the black leaders around him; Dr. King believed the civil rights movement should be based on non-violence.

Looking back on how he achieved it, one could only imagine how someone so young could meet with city, state, national and world leaders and not only hold his own but win them over. Let's be honest, Dr. King's education and intelligence didn't prepare him for the battles he would face. The wisdom he displayed could not have been learned; it had to be given to him by God for the job he was assigned to do. Dr. King realized the importance of media and the impact of television aiding their cause. And, most importantly, he realized that thirteen percent of the American Population, which was black, would not and could not; stand a chance against the most powerful police, national guard, and military force in the world. The only way to achieve the goals for the black citizens of America were to appeal to the God Conciseness of not only Americans but of world leaders who would witness the events as they unfolded on television.

This wisdom was God given and it was very effective. Most people never knew this but after his death; the doctor who performed the autopsy on Dr. King stated that although he was only thirty-nine years of age, he had a brain equal to a sixty- year old man. The wear and tear of the stress he was under affected him physically; however, God's grace was sufficient to see him through. Don't forget this wise statement, it is a fact; "blessed are the peacemakers, for they shall see God." Dr. King was perhaps the most influential peacemaker in the twentieth century. The United States of America is more united because of him.

After watching the abuses Dr. King was subjected to by individuals and organizations which were expecting the normal violent response whether physical or verbal: it is evident that Dr. King was given the gift of wisdom. On several occasions he discerned the end of his own life. Once he stated that he would die like Bobby Kennedy and in a famous speech he mentioned not making it to the promised land with the people he was serving. Longevity was important to him, but he knew it was not his destiny. Wisdom my brothers and sisters will show you things to come because Godly Wisdom: a spirit, isn't limited to time and space and neither is God.

CHAPTER THREE:
WISDOM'S PURPOSE

Wisdom carries two basic purposes or there are two sides to it. Proverbs 1:2, says; "to know wisdom and instruction; to perceive the words of understanding." In this verse the text's meaning of wisdom refers to "skill in living." It is used to refer to physical skills such as: tailoring, metalwork, woodwork, spinning, engraving, designing, building, and warfare. Used metaphorically, like in Proverbs, wisdom refers to the skill to live life successfully. In the very next verse wisdom takes on a totally different meaning:

> Proverbs 1:3, "to receive the instruction of wisdom, justice, and judgment, and equity."

The use of the word wisdom in this verse is a different Hebrew word which corresponds with a meaning centered around, good sense, wise dealings, and wise behavior. Ironically that is what the majority of parents focus on with their children and families.

Wisdom: Skill in Living

Wisdom is so important God Himself used her in creating the world which can be found in Proverbs 3:19, "The Lord by wisdom hath founded the earth, by understanding hath he established the heavens."

Now really, I don't need to say anything else concerning the importance of wisdom: if God uses wisdom, shouldn't we? Also, if God used wisdom in creating the world then this gives us even more evidence that God is not wisdom! By going back to the future we find hidden in Hebrews a scripture which will begin our look into this purpose for wisdom.

> *Hebrews 4:3, "For we which have believed do enter into rest, as he said, as I have sworn in my wrath. If they shall enter into my rest: although the work was finished from the foundation of the world."*

By focusing on the last sentence in this scripture there are two central themes relating to our subject of skill in living. The author gives us an insight into the power of God. From the foundation of the world, the work was finished. The key theme is work. One side of wisdom on a two-faced coin deals with works. All forms of works including physical, intellectual, monetary, creative, natural and spiritual are involved.

Earlier we learned that some of the Hebrews after leaving Egypt received the gift of wisdom to create or make everything related to the tabernacle. Naturally the Hebrews were craftsmen in the planning and construction of the roads, houses, bricks, pillars, jewelry, chariots, clothing, pyramids, and other structures throughout Egypt. In fact, Egypt lost all of its workforce and tradesmen when the Hebrew slaves left Egypt. No wonder Pharoah didn't want to let them go; who would do the work? Think about it, Egypt's entire workforce left in one day.

It is reasonable to conclude that two things most likely happened in relationship with the spirit of wisdom being given. First, wisdom enhanced or multiplied the skill level of certain men and women in order to meet the standards that God required for the tabernacle and its furnishings. Secondly, wisdom imparted talents in certain men and women which they did not have in order to meet the standards that God required. In other words they were all inspired or directed by the spirit of wisdom to some degree or another.

This skill of living or wisdom can even be found in warfare which is another category of skill in living. In fact, history has proven that during war, mankind experienced the most rapid advances in technology, medicine, and science then at any other time in history. The Old Testament or Old Covenant is full of scriptures depicting nations at war with the Hebrews or Israelites. Understandably, we are talking about a nation that is being born. A new nation made of ex-slaves from Egypt who had no experience in warfare.

The Hebrews were in the northern part of Egypt near the Nile River which was a very fertile section of the Egyptian Empire called Goshen. On their exodus from Egypt the Hebrews took the shortest route to the promised land called; "the way of the Philistines", a route or roadway the Philistines used to go to Egypt and vice versa. In the thirteenth chapter of Exodus, verses seventeen and eighteen, God led the people away from the land of the Philistines through the wilderness by the Red or Reed Sea due to the Hebrews becoming fearful when faced with the possibility of going to war with the Philistines.

To understand why, let's turn our attention to Jewish Historical sources. We never turn to the Jews to get an account of what happened to them, which is like asking Europeans about the American Civil Rights movement or asking Australians about American Indian History. So, why don't we go to the source if they are available? Nobody else knows about what happened to the Jews more in biblical times than the Jewish People who are still with us and have centuries of Ancient Jewish Sources like: the Tanaka or the Hebrew Bible; The Torah or the Pentateuch; The Mishnah which explains the Torah; The Upright Book (found in Joshua 10:13, 2 Samuel 1:18); and The Oral Law. Most Jewish Religious Leaders strongly believe that without The Oral Law, The Torah, Mishnah, and Tanaka cannot be properly understood.

Drawing from Jewish historians and books we can get a better picture of why God directed the Hebrews away from the way of the Philistines. According to the Jews, thirty years before the Exodus, Ephraim's descendants miscalculated the promise of four hundred years in Egypt. Some thirty thousand Hebrew men attempted the journey and fought against the Philistines who had decades of military experience. The Philistines destroyed the Hebrews and piled up their bones as a warning. God knew if the Hebrews saw these bones fear would overwhelm them, and they would want to return to Egypt. This adds to the Biblical account and explains why God led the Hebrews across the Red Sea and into the wilderness to reach the land of Canaan.

In the Old Testament, one of the best examples of God being involved in the lives of the Israelites can be seen in studying their war history. Wisdom comes into focus because there can be no debating the fact that the Israelites who were slaves in Egypt had no prior knowledge, experience, understanding, comprehension, or history to draw from when engaging other nations in war.

The Israelites faced nations whose armies were experienced on the battlefield and had governments and kingdoms for decades if not centuries. But the Israelites had a God who was fighting with them and throughout the Old Testament, scripture makes this fact known. In addition, the fear of their name was known to nations before they arrived due to God fighting with them in their battles. The most famous victory known is perhaps the fall of Jericho.

Wisdom at Jericho

The Children of Israel never suffered a defeat in battle against their enemies after leaving Egypt and their fame was known throughout the nations which can be seen in the battle of Jericho. In the second chapter of Joshua, spies were sent out to bring back an accurate report on the strengths and weaknesses of the city of Jericho.

The walls of Jericho were so massive that houses were on the top of the wall. A woman named Rahab and her family lived in such a house, and she hid the spies on her roof top. Rahab provides some very important information to the spies in the Joshua 2:9-11.

> *"And she said unto the men, I know that the Lord hath given you the land, and that your terror is fallen upon us, and that all the inhabitants of the land faint because of you. Because we have heard how the Lord hath dried up the water of the Red Sea for you, when you came out of the land of Egypt: and what you did to the two kings of the Amorites, that were on the other side of the Jordan, Sihon and Og, whom ye utterly destroyed. And as soon as we heard these things, our hearts did melt, neither did there remain any more courage in any*

man, because of you: for the Lord your God, he is God in heaven above and in earth beneath. "

Surprisingly, Rahab tells the spies that her country's military are already mentally and spiritually defeated because of the Israelites fame. The Bible records that the walls of Jericho came crashing down because of the obedience of the Israelites and the power of the Lord their God resulting in a tremendous victory. Jehovah God instructed Joshua to command the Hebrews to surround Jericho and walk around it multiple times without saying a word. Then on the final and seventh time, the priests blew trumpets, the Hebrews shouted collectively, and the walls fell down flat, leaving the city defenseless.

In addition, God commanded for the Hebrews to leave all the food or cattle and grain; thus, they were only permitted to take with them silver, gold, and vessels of brass and iron which would go into the treasury of the Lord and not the Hebrews' homes. Lastly, they were to burn the city.

Jericho was first excavated in 1868 by Charles Warren, in 1930 by John Garstan, and in the 1950's by Kathleen Kenyan. Excavation revealed two interesting details which collaborate the biblical account. First, throughout the city food storage bins and houses were overflowing with grains or food. Important because no military would leave a food supply untouched. But, God told Joshua not to take any food, only silver and gold from the city of Jericho. Secondly, the walls were found to have been destroyed by an earthquake and fire. Significant because the power of God caused the walls to fall, not man.

Interestingly enough, the sixth-day war in 1967 also known as the June War, which involved Egypt, Syria, Jordan and Iraq waging war against Israel with the intent of wiping Israel off the face of the earth; is a modern day miracle war depicting God being involved with Israel in battle. These Arab Nations declared war against Israel with The United States and Great Britain deciding to watch from the sidelines, thus leaving Israel all alone; but was Israel alone or was The Lord God-Jehovah with them? Egypt's President who led the Arab coalition was preparing a surprise attack and boarded a jet to command or oversee the war campaign by air. However, Israel decided to preemptively strike Egypt's air bases by flying low under radar and destroyed 500 jets and numerous air bases in 3 hours.

Meanwhile, the Egyptian President had informed Jordan that the Egyptian Air Forces had gained air superiority by repelling and defeating Israel's Air Forces, while unaware of Israel's surprise attack. In the confusion there was misinformation being communicated by the Arab coalition due to Israel's surprise attacks. After gaining air supremacy Israel ground forces led by their tanks continued reaping havoc on the Arab Coalition. A war that started at 4 o'clock am on the 5th of June, ended six days later on the 11th of June, with a cease fire being signed due to the overwhelming battlefield losses suffered by the Arab Coalition, leaving the world stunned by the speed of their victory.

No one expected Israel to win this war, not when you consider their war experience and military power compared to the Arabs. By the numbers, Arabs had 2 times more troops. Arabs had 5 times more tanks (5,000 vs. 1,000). Arabs had 4 times more aircraft (900 vs. 196). Egypt alone lost 65 percent of its military power. Egypt lost 500 jets in the first 3 hours. The Arab Coalition lost almost ½ of its tanks. The Arab Coalition lost 20,000 troops compared to 1,000 Israeli troops. No wonder this war is called the 6th Day Miracle War. God proved to the world through Israel that he is a God of War and The Lord is his name, Exodus 15:3. Afterall, Israel became a nation in 1948 even though they neither had experience on the battlefield, the numbers in troops, nor weaponry to defeat the coalition of Arab nations who possessed both.

The reason why war is used relates to the fact that we are in a spiritual war with the kingdom of Satan and our weapons are not carnal, but mighty through God to the pulling down of strongholds: casting down imaginations, and every high thing that exalteth itself against the knowledge of God, and bringing into captivity every thought to the obedience of Christ (1 Corinthians 10:4-5).

Under the Old Covenant or Testament, the Children of Israel fought natural enemies, but under the New Covenant or Testament the Children of God's battle is spiritual.

Ephesians 6:10-18: "Finally, my brethren, be strong in the Lord and in the power of his might. Put on the whole armor of God, that ye may be able to stand against the wiles of the devil. For we wrestle not against flesh and blood, but against principalities, against powers, against the rulers of darkness of this world, against spiritual wickedness in high places. Wherefore take unto you the whole armor of God that ye may be able to withstand in the evil day, and having done all, to stand. Stand therefore, having your loins girt about with truth, and having on the breastplate of righteousness; and your feet shod with the preparation of the gospel of peace: Above all, taking the shield of faith, wherewith ye shall be able to quench all the fiery darts of the wicked. And take the helmet of salvation and the sword of the Spirit, which is the word of God: praying always with all prayer and supplication in the Spirit, and watching thereunto with all perseverance and supplication for all saints. "

In either case one thing is certain! Without God, we can do nothing! The skills that mankind have acquired, invented, used, and rely on to improve our daily lives or help us achieve an expected end; are often attributed to someone who asked for and used wisdom for help.

Wisdom: Operating in Lives

The second purpose of wisdom is applying her in our daily lives. Wisdom's motive is to impart or guide someone with instructions or truths that will stand the test of time. True wisdom leads a person to a perspective that will stand the test of time throughout eternity. Her goal is based on two simple scriptures. For the beginning of wisdom is to fear God and keep his commandments which are the sole or whole duty of mankind; and, to love the Lord your God with all your mind, heart, strength and soul and love your neighbor as yourself. Wisdom leads a person through the difficulties of life in this world while preparing him or her to enter the gates of heaven. Therefore, we should be quick to hear and slow to speak because even a fool is considered as wise who can control his tongue or knows when to shut up.

In this sense, wisdom gives a person a choice. By using wisdom, a person decides to be seen as wise, and by not choosing her a person will act foolishly, in most cases without even realizing it. The aim is for a person to inculcate wisdom into their life which will guide the moral discipline of that person thus leading to an abundant and successful life. This side of wisdom deals with the areas of a person's life such as: family, death, life, discretion, enemies, friends, eating, the heart or mind, the home, labor, law, lazy people, love, lust, neighbors, peace, pride, poverty, riches, prayer, righteousness, sex, sin, shame, sleep, soul, body, spirit, the tongue, trust, wine, the wicked, time, women, and words. So, a person who possesses wisdom should have - wise behavior, wise dealings, or good sense. When I was growing up they called it common sense, but common sense isn't that common, is it?

Rahab finds Wisdom

There is a person who draws little attention by historians, theologians, scholars, and clergy even though this person's deeds exemplify one of the most amazing stories relating to faith that can be found in the Bible. Maybe it's because this person is a woman or isn't an Israelite. There can be no denying the fact that the Bible was written by men at a time and in a society where women were considered as second-class citizens. No matter the reason, God saw and honored her faith which gained her entrance into the Bible and the faiths' hall of fame. We are going to go back to the wall of Jericho and take a closer look at a woman named Rahab. Rahab was a citizen of Jericho, a city located in the land of Canaan, who is one of a handful of biblical legends that made their way into the Book of Hebrews, known as faiths' hall of fame. Rahab can be found in Hebrews 11:31.

"By faith the harlot Rahab perished not with them that believed not, when she received the spies with peace."

Drawing from the scripture, the first thing that jumps out at the reader is the fact that Rahab is a harlot. A woman who sells her body for money as a means of support. But how is it that a prostitute is honored by God above all the righteous men and women in the Bible who didn't make it into faiths' hall of fame. One answer is found in James 2:21-25.

"Was not Abraham our father justified by works, when he had offered Isaac his son upon the altar. Seest thou how faith wrought with his works, and by works was faith made perfect? And the scripture was fulfilled which saith, Abraham Believed God, and it was imputed or counted unto him for righteousness: and he was called, the Friend of God. Ye see then how that by works a man is justified, and not by faith only. Likewise, also was not Rahab the harlot justified by works, when she had received the messengers, and had sent them out another way?"

We always hear about Abraham's act of faith being counted for righteousness but never Rahab's. In all actuality, she demonstrated the same boldness in words and deeds as Abraham demonstrated. What is even more impressive about Rahab is that she was a prostitute or one of the lowest citizens of a Gentile City condemned by God, whose newfound faith in the Hebrew God was brought to life by her words and works. Their faith was based upon the fact that the Messiah was coming while today our faith looks back at the cross.

Another reason why Rahab is so amazing surrounds her place in history. According to the Bible she married Salmon and they had a son named Boaz who married Ruth. Boaz and Ruth were the parents of Obed, the father of Jesse, who was the father of King David, which can be found in Matthew, chapter one, verses 5 and 6. So, Rahab is in the lineage of King David and Jesus.

Finally, is her appearance in the Book of Joshua where she steps into the pages of history through the door of faith. It was an ordinary day in Jericho until the two spies sent by Joshua entered Jericho. Of all the citizens living in Jericho, somehow the spies ended up at Rahab's house. Rahab lived with her father and mother along with her brothers and sisters which was a common practice for families during that period. The house was located on top of the walls of Jericho which illustrates how massive the walls of Jericho were.

The city was strategically located for both military and economic reasons making Jericho an important city for the land of Canaan, which would explain the need for such a massive wall. Rahab knowingly and willingly accepted the spies into her home. She faced a possible death sentence for helping, lodging, and aiding enemies of the state. Not only was Rahab facing these charges and a possible death sentence; her whole family or household which included Rahab's mother, father, sisters and brothers would suffer the consequences of her decision. And, true to form, Rahab's neighbors got word back to the King of Jericho that the spies were seen entering her house. Either before the king's men arrived or while they were at the door, Rahab took the two spies to the roof and hid them. As expected, the king sent his men to Rahab's house who informed her that the spies were seen entering her house. She was given an opportunity to tell the King's men where the spies were or face the consequences. Rahab was faced with a life-or-death dilemma that required an immediate response.

With Rahab's family and herself, facing the threat of treason against her own country; Rahab conspired to hide the spies on her roof. She lied to the King's men and said that although the two spies came into her house, they left, and she didn't know where they went. She suggested that the King's Men should pursue after the spies because they most likely fled the city. Afterwards Rahab returned to the rooftop and revealed information to the spies that would help the Children of Israel defeat her own city, Jericho.

This leads us into one of the most miraculous stories in the Bible, especially when you take into account the fact that Rahab was a harlot: was not educated; was a woman living in the middle east in ancient times; was not married; and didn't come from a wealthy or influential family. Then there is the mouth dropping truth that Rahab was raised in a world that worshiped multiple pagan gods. So, it is a real wonder how this young woman came to trust in the God of Abraham, Isaac and Jacob? And where did the wisdom come from in her dealings with the spies? Somehow and someway Rahab knew without any prior knowledge that the spies would keep the oath, or covenant with Rahab by saving her family from death because of the coming invasion. Rahab showed more faith in the spies God than she did in the nation and gods of Jericho.

In Joshua 2:8-18, we find her thoughts on full display:

> *"And before they (the spies) were laid down, Rahab came up unto them upon the roof, and she said unto the men, I know that the Lord hath given you the land, and that your terror is fallen upon us, and that all the inhabitants of the land faint because of you; For we have heard how the Lord dried up the water of the Red Sea for you, when ye came out of Egypt, and what ye did unto the two kings of the Amorites, who were on the other side of the Jordan River, Sihon and Og, whom ye utterly destroyed. And as soon as we had heard these things, our hearts did melt, neither did there remain any more courage in any man, because of you, for the Lord your God, he is God in heaven above, and in the earth beneath, now therefore, I pray you, swear unto me by the Lord, since I have shewed you kindness unto my father's house, and give me a true token; And that ye will save alive my father, and my mother, and my brethren, and my sisters, and all that they*

have, and deliver our lives from death; And the men answered her, Our life for yours, if ye utter not this our business. And it shall be, when the Lord hath given us the land, that we will deal kindly and truly with thee."

Now we know that faith cometh by hearing and hearing by the word of God is the vehicle that converted Rahab's pagan faith to her faith and belief in the God of Abraham, Isaac and Jacob; she said, "We heard how the Lord dried up the water of the Red Sea for you, and that we heard about all your victories." But what is so amazing is her proclamation, which shows us that God was dealing with her. Rahab should not have known that their God was the God of heaven above and all the earth. Evidently, the Spirit of Wisdom imparted this everlasting revelation in her. From her first encounter with the spies, when they left and upon their return, Rahab dealt wisely with them. Wisdom must have spoken to her because she knew that the spies did not just happen to show up at her house out of all the houses in Jericho.

Furthermore, this was the chance of a lifetime and she had just one opportunity to take advantage of it. Understanding that this opportunity would not come her way again, she took full advantage of it. Rahab took the lead and initiated the conversation leading to an oath or promise thus saving her whole household. But she did not know anything about the spies or their God, yet the way Rahab dealt with the spies was very wise. After hiding the spies and informing them about the fear that God had placed in the hearts of Jericho, Rahab informed the spies that she wanted to enter an oath, promise or covenant with not only them, but with their God. And, who told Rahab that the God of Abraham, Isaac and Jacob was a covenant-making God. There is no indication that the relationship between the God of Abraham, Isaac, and Jacob was given to her by the spies or by God, which leaves the spirit of Wisdom revealing this truth causing Rahab to use it to her benefit, and for the Lord God's purpose.

There is one thing about Rahab that sticks out like a sore thumb in this story and apparently the spies didn't suspect a thing: she was orchestrating the whole thing. Not only did Rahab send the king's men on the trail of the two spies while they were on her roof top, but without any military experience she told the spies to wait until night and hide in the hills for three days and then it would be safe to return to the Israelite encampment. Taking no chance of her neighbors seeing anything, the spies escaped by night by a scarlet or red rope from the great wall of Jericho near Rahab's house. The same rope representing the blood was to be placed in her window to save everyone inside when God would destroy the city with the aid of the Israelites. Rahab acted harmless like a dove, and wise like a serpent. The wisdom shown by Rahab was not the byproduct of prior knowledge, teachings or understanding that she possessed; hence it doesn't fit into the definition of wisdom that we have been taught.

The Lord God led the two spies to a cunning woman named Rahab, and they had no clue that the Lord had arranged it. With the assistance of Wisdom, Rahab did the rest. So, when the might of men can't get the job done; where armies fail and money ends; surprisingly the educated get lost, and the fast and furious fall short; as the will of mankind falls short, and technology breaks down, the days begin to come to an end, and time suddenly runs out...there is a scripture in the Bible that is calling us to: "Thus, saith the Lord of Hosts, consider ye, and call for the mourning women, that they may come, And Send For The Cunning Women, that they may come." Jeremiah 9:17.

Or those who have the spirit of Wisdom to see the end from the beginning. One thing is certain about Rahab; she was a gentile woman and wisdom helped her gain access into the faith's hall of fame and the lineage of both King David and Jesus The Christ.

CHAPTER FOUR:
THREE SOURCES OF WISDOM

The Old Testament, or Covenant, or Pentateuch, or Torah are the best places to find the definition for the word Wisdom. Ironically, all these Biblical Books are written in the Hebrew language which is where we see the first mention of the word. Likewise, Wisdom is used more in these books than in the New Testament or Covenant. The word Wisdom in these books comes from the Hebrew word, "Chokma." Chokma is spelled with the Hebrew letters or pictures: Chet, Kaf, Mem and Tav. Chet is a picture of a sanctuary or hidden place, Kaf is a picture of a hand which means cover or uncover, Mem is a picture of living waters, Tav is a picture which means mark.

Further definitions deal with discernment, insight,experience, skill in living, one who separates. But the most compelling revelation concerning this Hebrew word is that "Chokma" is a grammatically feminine noun. In other words, Wisdom or "Chokma" in the Old Testament/Covenant or Pentateuch, or Torah isn't a *he* or an *it*, but a *she*. What has been in plain sight but hidden centers around Wisdom or "Chokma" being a feminine pronoun. This is not surprising when you consider that God is a Spirit and he created both male and female; therefore God is as much female as he is male because both came out of Him! Then there are angels that are both male and female beings created by God. Next the Bible mentions spirits and the seven spirits we discussed earlier of which Wisdom is found. Therefore, when we combine what we have learned thus far the evidence is indisputable that Wisdom is a "female spirit."

In the movie *Scrooge: A Christmas Carol*, one of the most popular Christmas movies ever, the ghost of Christmas past is a female. So why is it so unthinkable to consider that a spirit in the Bible can't be a female. Well, "Chokma " is and "Her Name Is Wisdom." Further evidence can be found in the New Testament/Covenant which was not written in Hebrew but in Greek. In the Greek language the word Wisdom comes from the word, "Sophia" or "Sofia" which means: cleverness, skill, common sense, insight and right application. What is so amazing concerning this Greek word "Sophia" is that it's a pronoun that is feminine or female just like in the Hebrew. The preponderance of evidence is overwhelming. Both the Hebrew and Greek; or Old Testament and New Testament nouns for the word Wisdom is feminine or Female. It is clear from what has been presented and uncovered thus far reveals that God wants us to know that, "Wisdom is a Female Spirit."

Godly Wisdom

The Bible makes it clear that there exists three sources from where Wisdom comes from or to be politically correct; there are three very different types of Wisdom that a person can have. The first type comes from above. This Wisdom is called Godly Wisdom. Then there is earthly Wisdom. Finally, we have devilish or satanic Wisdom. James, the brother of Jesus, is one of the few books in the Bible where these three sources of Wisdom are seen together in the same verse.

James 3:15-17 reads: "This Wisdom descendeth not from above, but is earthly, sensual, devilish; for where envying and strife is, there is confusion and every evil work, but the Wisdom that is from above is first pure, then peaceable, gentle, and easy to be entreated, full of mercy and good fruits, without partiality, and without hypocrisy."

By taking a closer look at the scripture James is showing the differences between the three types of Wisdoms which are striking. In verse thirteen he asks a question leading the reader into the focal point of the conversation which is true and false Wisdom. "Who is a wise man or and endued with knowledge among you? Let him show out of a good conversation or lifestyle his works with the meekness of Wisdom."

James is pointing out that a person needs to examine themselves first and determine if their motives and heart line up with the word of God. The answer is simple enough; we are to treat our brothers and sisters including neighbors as ourselves. And we are to love the Lord our God with all our heart, strength, mind and soul while loving our neighbors as ourselves. In addition, James challenges the reader to take inventory of one of the main ingredients associated with Godly Wisdom or True Wisdom which is being and doing good in all manner of your life, like Jesus. The scriptures tell us that Jesus "went about doing good" because of Love!

The next three verses shine a spotlight on the ingredients found in the two wisdoms that are not of God; therefore, these two wisdoms' (man's and the devil's) show signs of being manufactured differently. So, when there are signs of bitterness, envying, strife, lying, confusion, evil, sensual or seducing spirits, wars, fighting, lusts, partiality or respect of persons', jealousy, adultery, fornication, pride, self- gratification and exaltation, greed or a sinful conversation/lifestyle: then the Spirit of the wisdom being displayed doesn't come from above or God. This wisdom comes from either the spirit of the world/man, or the spirit of Satan. The Spirit of Godly Wisdom or True Wisdom embraces the truth and is clothed in love and humility. Godly Wisdom is pure and promotes peace, ending with a fruit that embodies righteousness.

Some verses like 1 Corinthians 2:4-7, show the contrast of Wisdom's two sources. Here you will find these words where Paul is trying to convey the differences of two types of Wisdom. "And my speech and my preaching was not with enticing words of man's wisdom, but in the demonstration of the Spirit and of power; That your faith should not stand in the wisdom of men, but in the power of God; Howbeit we speak Wisdom among them that are perfect, yet not the wisdom of this world, nor of the princes of this world, that come to naught; But we speak the wisdom of God in a mystery, even the hidden Wisdom, which God ordained before the world unto our glory."

Pulling from this scripture leads us into the original or true source of Wisdom called Godly Wisdom. She was ordained before the creation of the world to be used by God for creation and by his creation or mankind. She was the first and only source of Wisdom created by God. Adding Proverbs 8:22, (Jesus or God possessed or used Wisdom in the beginning of his way, before his work of old), gives further evidence that this type of Wisdom comes from God and is the true source created and used by God. The spirit of Wisdom separates good from evil; she speaks truth and wickedness and lies are an abomination unto her, the words preceding from her lips are righteousness: she gives instructions and knowledge. Wisdom dwells with prudence, kindness, meekness and humility: she is the source of witty inventions; counsel and strength are hers; kings reign because of her; judges are given instruction from her, the fruits of wisdom are better than silver and fine gold; her ways lead to everlasting life: order is the nature of wisdom; she hangs out with The Father, Son and Holy Spirit; and she is knocking at the door of your heart to let her in!

Godly Wisdom was set up in eternity, from the beginning or before earth was. There was no earth, or fields, nor the highest parts of the dust of the earth. When he prepared the heavens and established the clouds above, and strengthened the fountains of the deep; when he gave the sea orders and established the foundations of the earth, The Spirit of Wisdom was there. She was by God, as one brought up with him, and was his daily delight, rejoicing always before him, and the delight of Wisdom were the sons and daughters of men. She is crying out for her children to have a relationship with her and to hear the instructions that will make one wise. Blessed is the person that heareth her and practices her ways. For whoso finds Wisdom findeth life and shall obtain favor of the Lord.

Wisdom carries the higher perspective by which God understands and sees things that a man or woman is incapable of. For Christians she gives the purpose and meaning of life, while showing us the way to eternal life. One of the most inspirational verses involving the purpose of wisdom can be found in another book that Solomon and Moses took part in writing, Psalms. Psalms is mostly attributed to King David, however the book lists a total of six different authors. The three mentioned are the most famous, while; Asaph, Heman, and Ethan are basically unknown.

Psalms 104:24, "O Lord, how manifold are thy works! In wisdom hast thou made them all: the earth is full of thy riches."

In the beginning of time or dating back to the creation in the book of Genesis, wisdom was there with God the Father, God the Son, and God the Holy Spirit; or what we call the Trinity. Wisdom's purpose as displayed in this verse is to help in the planning, building and completion of the world or God's creation.

Wisdom also helps in designing and maintaining order which is beauty in the eyes of The Lord. Nature, which includes such things as the weather, science, astrology, rivers, oceans, atoms, protons etc., have an order to them or what we call patterns. There are pathways or currents in the ocean. There are patterns with the wind or air which can be studied. Outer space has a noticeable effect on our bodies and the earth. Plants take in carbon dioxide and produce oxygen. The ice in the South and North Poles stabilize our weather. Soil contains nutrients which are vital to sustain life.

There is a code, DNA or compound for everything from water-h20, to mankind. In short, everything that we both see and don't see is governed by a purpose and a pattern having an order. Is it possible that previous generations who had less machines and technology to help them perform their work relied on wisdom more than we do today because they knew they needed help to accomplish the things that we look back at and marvel at. For instance, there are the seven wonders of the world. The pyramids are precise building achievements: ancient underground waterways built by man through solid rock that started at two ends of a mountain and met in the middle—hieroglyphics with paint that baffle scientists in their longevity.

Today we rely on technology and machines more than we do each other. Mankind seeks after technology and spends more and more time with his creation. We can be in a place full of people without anyone communicating or interacting with one another, because everyone's on their cell phones, iPad or laptops. Simply stated, people are communicating or interacting with their devices. So, where does that leave time for wisdom or God for that matter?

The second part of the text suggests that wisdom has another purpose, which is to give insight into the things that are valuable; both naturally and spiritually. Adam must have possessed wisdom when naming God's creation and distinguishing the difference between gold and a rock. Likewise, we need wisdom in determining the value of things both naturally and spiritually. Seeing we are a body, soul and spirit creation.

Godly Wisdom comes to lead us through the dark and stormy times of life just like when Paul found himself in a hurricane or typhoon and all hope that he would be saved was taken away by the storm which was surrounding him; but word came to Paul by an angel sent by God that he would make it to dry land on broken pieces because he must make it to Rome. Likewise wisdom helps Christians make it to heaven.

There are numerous ways for a person to receive Wisdom. Again, James the brother of Jesus, lets us know: "If any of you lack Wisdom, let him ask of God, that giveth to all men liberally, and upbraideth not; and it shall be given him" (James 1:5).

This scripture records a simple way for people to receive Godly Wisdom; just ask God! By dissecting this verse we find that God gives Wisdom to any man, woman, boy or girl liberally without prejudice or respect of person, but sound wisdom mentioned in the book of Proverbs, the second chapter verse seven, is laid up or set aside for the righteous.

The When of Wisdom

It makes sense that Wisdom was created by God when he created the hosts of heaven such as: Beasts, Archangels, Angels, Spirits, and Seraphim. We know that Wisdom predates the Bible because of scriptures like Proverbs 8:22, "The Lord possessed me in the beginning of his way, before his works of old."

Surprisingly verse 30 gives even a better insight into the essence and beginnings of Wisdom; "Then I was by him as one brought up with him, and I was daily his delight, rejoicing always before him." Wisdom reveals to the reader that she is close to God and spends a lot of time hanging out with God. And most importantly Wisdom says that she is as one brought up with God. What a mind-blowing perspective. Wisdom is giving us a look into her past and beginnings with God. Wisdom is clearly declaring that she was raised in the same household of God and shares an intimate relationship with God that resembles that of a family member.

This brings us to King Solomon who became king over the nation of Israel and was King David's Son. When he took the throne of his father David he prayed to the Lord and asked for something very strange. He wanted to receive sound wisdom to judge the Nation of Israel. God granted Solomon's request for Wisdom and added natural blessings because he didn't ask for anything for himself, but to the contrary, his heart was set on being able to lead God's people. The story of Solomon's Wisdom is one of the most popular ancient accounts in the Bible relating to Wisdom. Not only that, but he is still considered as the wisest man other than Jesus who ever lived.

Yet, what have we really learned or taken away from this story after all these years? When considering a person who is wise, without debate King Solomon comes to mind. The Wisdom he manifested was so great in his time that the Queen of Sheba traveled from Ethiopia to prove him because she heard of his fame. After meeting King Solomon and witnessing his acts and wisdom she made this stunning statement: "Howbeit I believed not their words which I heard in mine own land of thine acts, and of thy wisdom. Howbeit I believed not their words, until I came, and mine eyes had seen it, and behold the one half of the greatness of thy wisdom was not told me, for thou exceedest the fame that I heard."

King Solomon is known for providing us with the first Temple of Israel that housed the famous Ark of the Covenant and the largest collection of proverbs and poems. He was not only blessed with True Wisdom, but God gave him great wealth, riches and fame, resulting in a man who was one of the richest men of his time. This is important since today we relate Wisdom with prosperity and fame. In other words, we believe a wise person is blessed with prosperity, or is rich, or is famous, or holds a title/position; likewise, most Christians, Jews, Islamic, Buddhist, Hindu's believe a poor person cannot be wise!

The Forgotten Poor Wise Man

This Biblical story has never been preached, or taught, or discussed, or even brought up because the person who performed these miraculous feats was poor. Hidden in the Book of Ecclesiastes Chapter 9, verses fourteen through eighteen, is the account of a poor wise man, forgotten by men, but not by God!

"There was a little city, and few men within it, and there came a great king against it, and besieged it, and built great bulwarks, or snares, or strongholds against it; Now there was found in it a poor wise man, and he by his wisdom delivered the city, yet no man remembered that same poor man: Then said I, Wisdom is better than strength, nevertheless, the poor man's wisdom is despised, and his words are not heard, The words of the wise men are heard in quiet more than the cry of him that ruleth among fools; Wisdom is better than weapons of war, but one sinner destroyeth much good."

Despite the value of Wisdom, she often goes unheeded and unnoticed because of whom it comes from. If Wisdom doesn't come from someone who we believe is wise by our definition; then it is often overlooked. And God forbid if a person has a character flaw or is subject to making a mistake in their life, like other men and women. Compared to other great men and women in the Bible, why isn't this man remembered? He went to work every day. He was a good citizen and provided for his family. When the enemy came to destroy the city, instead of fleeing, hiding or falling into the shadows depending on someone else who was responsible for protecting the city to take the lead, the poor wise man stood up and presented a plan to the leaders, and took charge of the military leading to a miraculous victory. And instead of reaping the rewards of his victory. Instead of becoming a national hero. This poor wise man did not seek fame or riches, but desired to go back to his normal faithful life. What is even more miraculous than the victory is the fact that his city, which was delivered by his hands, forgot all about him. Why? Because he was poor; not because he was wise but due to him not fitting their definition of who a successful man or wise person is!

Man's Worldly Wisdom

The second source of Wisdom is earthly, natural or of man. Apostle Pauls' first letter to the Corinthian Church was written from Ephesus and deals with two types of Wisdom early in the writing. Twice, Paul mentions the contrary natures of two types of Wisdom; Godly and Worldly. The first appearance can be found in 1 Corinthians, chapter 1: verses 19 through 27:

"For it is written, I will destroy the wisdom of the wise and will bring to nothing the understanding of the prudent, where is the wise? Where is the scribe? Where is the disputer of this world? Hath not God made foolish the wisdom of this world? For after that in the wisdom of God, the world by wisdom knew not God, it pleased God by the foolishness of preaching to save them that believe; For the Jews require a sign, and the Greeks seek after wisdom; But we preach Christ crucified, unto the Jews a stumbling block, and unto the Greeks' foolishness: But unto them which are called, both Jews and Greeks, Christ the power of God, and the wisdom of God, because the foolishness of God is wiser than men; and the weakness of God is stronger than men; For ye see your calling, brethren, how that not many wise men after the flesh, not many mighty, not many noble, are called; but God hath chosen the foolish things of the world to confound the wise, and God hath chosen the weak things of the world to confound the things which are mighty, And base things of the world, and things which are despised, hath God chosen, yea, and things which are not, to bring to naught things that are that no flesh should glory in his presence."

Before diving into these scriptures and showing the differences between Godly Wisdom and worldly Wisdom; the origin of worldly, or man's Wisdom must be investigated and there is no better place to begin than in the Book of the beginning, which is Genesis. So, put a thumbtack here, and we will return.

There is hidden in the pages of Genesis a revealing story of the beginning of worldly or man's wisdom. But if the truth be told, it has always been in plain sight. The one thing which caused Adam and Eve to eat of the tree has been overlooked. They were not trying to eat off the tree to live forever or gain eternal life. As a matter of fact, Adam and Eve weren't even interested in the tree in the midst of the Garden until Satan, disguised as a serpent, entered the Garden. When they were created, the only thing that God had programmed them with, was to know good. Their hearts were pure and innocent because they were neither introduced to sin nor born with a sinful nature. This is brought to light right after the fall when God pronounced punishment upon mankind, the serpent, and the earth disobeying his word.

After God performed the first sacrifice in order to cover the sin which Adam and Eve had committed, he covered them with the skins of the slain animal. There in the twenty- second verse of the third chapter of Genesis, God said, "Behold, the man has become as one of us to know good and evil." This perspective from God proves that Adam and Eve had no knowledge regarding sin, righteousness, or Satan's intentions.

Adam and Eve were undoubtedly out of their league when confronting Satan. Satan is such a master at manipulation and deceit that Adam and Eve had no clue that their actions were influenced by Satan's thoughts. In fact, his thoughts became their thoughts and they didn't even know it. The origin of mans' worldly wisdom is first found in Genesis 2:17, where it says, "But of the tree of the knowledge of good and evil, thou shalt not eat of it: for in the day that thou eatest thereof thou shalt surely die." The key in this verse is the tree of the knowledge of good and evil. What does it mean? The search takes us to verse 5 which says, "For God doth know that in the day ye eat thereof, then your eyes shall be opened, and ye shall be as gods, knowing good and evil."

Most people focus on the phrase that "ye shall be as gods or become like gods," while ignoring the most important phrase which follows: "knowing good and evil." Apparently, knowing good and evil will make them like gods, so what does that mean, exactly? The answer can be found in the very next verse and is given by Eve in her response to the serpent.

Verse 6 clearly explains that "[And] when the woman saw that the tree was good for food, and that it was pleasant to the eyes, and a tree to be desired To Make One Wise, she took of the fruit thereof, and did eat, and gave also unto her husband with her, and he did eat." The phrase to know good and evil in previous verses have been replaced by the true meaning of the phrase which is Wisdom. There is no disputing the fact Adam and Eve ate the fruit because they wanted to get Wisdom! And there can be no debating the obvious, to know good and evil means to have Wisdom.

God didn't want them to experience the Wisdom that the tree provided because this Wisdom was inferior and earthly. The type of Wisdom offered by the tree was contrary to Godly Wisdom and would cause Adam and Eve to flee from their Creator instead of drawing closer to him which is what Godly Wisdom does. This truth was played out in verse 8; "And they heard the voice of the Lord God walking in the garden in the cool of the day, And Adam and Eve Hid Themselves from The Presence Of the Lord God Amongst the Trees of The Garden."

This Wisdom made Adam and Eve believe they could hide themselves from the God who created not only them, but the whole planet and galaxy they were living in. This is why God didn't want them to eat the fruit of the tree. God knew the fruit of this earthly wisdom would cause mankind to reject the very existence of God because one of earthly wisdom's characteristics is to reject the existence of God the Creator. Earthly Wisdom then infects the soul into believing that they don't need God because they are gods.

So, why did God put this fruit in the garden in the first place is not made known in scriptures. Maybe it was to prove Mankind, or to test their obedience to him. No matter the reason, one thing is certain, The Lord God knew what Adam and Eve would do before he created them which is manifested in Revelation 13:8, "And all that dwell upon the earth shall worship him, whose names are not written in the book of life of The Lamb Slain From the Foundation of The World." By digesting earthly wisdom which was wrapped in fruit: Adam and Eve, allowed this type of wisdom to be released into the earth. The result is known as worldly, earthly, or manly wisdom.

This type of Wisdom is designed to meet the needs of things pertaining to this world which includes: mankind, animals, birds, fish, the planet and atmosphere, the solar system, and our fleshly desires. Additionally, worldly/earthly or manly wisdom never was intended for eternal or Godly purposes therefore it is void of God's point of view. This Wisdom's purpose is intended for life on this earth and promoting man as the god of this earth; resulting in an ideology that God the Creator doesn't exist.

Now let's retrieve the thumbtack and return to 1 Corinthians 1:19-27 with what has been learned about worldly/earthly or manly Wisdom. A lot of material in 1 Corinthians has been covered already, so, the focus going forward will lean towards a brief recap and illuminating statements in scriptures that haven't been expounded on.

Verse 19 starts with an alarming prediction given by The Lord God regarding man's wisdom, "I will destroy the wisdom of the wise." Because man's wisdom was not intended to be released on the earth and leads mankind away from God. Because man's wisdom fights against the Wisdom of God which he had intended for man, God promises to destroy man's wisdom at a preordained appointed time.

With that being said, until that happens the war between Godly Wisdom and earthly, worldly or man's wisdom will continue with the superior Godly Wisdom continuing to show there is no comparison between the two whenever they face each other.

The scriptures illustrate the fact that man's wisdom is foolishness in the eyes of God because it refuses to recognize the existence of God the Creator. So, God in his Wisdom has chosen the simple, weak, foolish and base things of this world to confound the wisdom of man which sees these attributes as worthless. God the Creator purposely selected or designed these things along with Jesus' death on the cross to silence the wisdom of man.

We don't have to go far for the next scripture regarding the comparisons between Godly and manly Wisdom. In the second chapter of First Corinthians: verses 4 through 6; we find Paul comparing Godly Wisdom with worldly Wisdom again: "And my speech and my preaching was not with enticing words of man's Wisdom, but in demonstration of the Spirit and of power; That your faith should not stand in the Wisdom of men, but in the power of God; Howbeit we speak Wisdom among them that are perfect(mature): Yet not the Wisdom of this world, nor of the princes of this world, that come to naught; But we speak the Wisdom of God in a mystery, even the hidden Wisdom, which God ordained before the world unto our glory."

Where a person places their faith is vital to the struggle between the wisdom of this world and Godly Wisdom, because the placement of one's faith will determine if one will ever know the purpose for their life that God has already planned for them in this life. Furthermore, Godly Wisdom will lead a person to eternal life with God the Creator, while the wisdom of men only concerns earthly values and purposes. Man's wisdom entices the flesh of mankind to focus on themselves as godlike beings causing man to believe that they are in control of their lives and this world. Simply put, this wisdom has not changed from the days of Adam and Eve. Remember that Adam and Eve did not seek to find God after they disobeyed God in the Garden of Eve, instead they hid themselves, resulting in God looking for Adam and Eve.

Satan's Wisdom

The third type of wisdom mentioned in the Bible is devilish or satanic wisdom. In order to get a good understanding of its design and purpose we must get insight into the Devil or Satan. Many ignorantly believe that Satan who is known by other names such as: Lucifer, Devil, Morning Star, Fallen Cherub, Serpent, Accuser of the brethren, Beelzebub, Belial, Enemy, Dragon, Father of lies, Tempter, Deceiver, Evil One, Ruler of this world, Prince of the air, and god of this age; is more than a fallen angel or heavenly host created by God but he is not! He was responsible for leading a third of the angels who were in heaven to rebel against God resulting in their expulsion. Jesus said he beheld Satan as lightning falling from heaven. He appeared in the Garden of Eden as a serpent tricking Adam and Eve to eat the fruit of the forbidden tree.

He showed up while Jesus was beginning his public ministry in the wilderness after fasting and praying for forty days as the Tempter. He hates God and anything that God loves which includes mankind. Now let's take a good look at some of the things he (Satan) is responsible for which includes the following: wars, lusts, killing, murders, adultery, fornication, pride, envy, deceit, covetousness, wickedness, maliciousness, debate, lying, whisperers, backbiters, despitefulness, boasting, uncleanness, inventor of evil, disobedient, unnatural affection, implacable, death, unmercifulness, theft, illness, sickness and sin. All these traits or ungodly behaviors are a direct result of the influence and nature of Satan or the Devil. By examining Satan's or Lucifer's deeds, acts and works one can determine his motives and character. According to the scripture both mankind and the heavenly host which includes angels were created by God with a free will. Even Satan or Lucifer was created by God which can be found in the Book of Ezekiel.

Ezekiel 28:13-17, "Thou has been in Eden the garden of God, every precious stone was thy covering, the sardius, topaz, and the diamond, the beryl, the onyx, and the jasper, the sapphire, the emerald, and the carbuncle, and gold: the workmanship of thy tabrets and of thy pipes was prepared in thee in the day that thou was created. Thou art the anointed cherub that covereth, and I have set thee so, thou wast upon the holy mountain of God, thou hast walked up and down in the midst of the stones of fire; thou wast perfect in thy ways from the day that thou wast created, till iniquity was found in thee; by the multitude of thy merchandise they have filled the midst of thee with violence, and thou hast sinned, therefore I will destroy thee, O covering cherub, from the midst of the stones of fire; thine heart was lifted up because of thy beauty, thou hast corrupted thy wisdom by reason of thy brightness, I will cast thee to the ground, I will lay thee before kings, that they may behold thee. "

The scripture mentions several things about Satan that are very interesting: Satan was a beautiful cherub that was covered in precious stones. There were tabrets and pipes in him pointing to his unmatched musical ability. He was created to cover the holy of holies with his wings. He was a high-ranking cherub which gave him access to the mountain of God. He was perfect in his ways. Iniquity was found in him. Because of his greatness his heart became filled with violence and sin. He was lifted up with pride because of his beauty. He corrupted the Wisdom of God by looking at his brightness, fame and position. Thus, Satan's wisdom was created.

Getting right to the point without sugar coating anything, this look over scripture verifies what Jesus stated when he said that he beheld Satan as lightning falling from heaven. After Satan who wanted to not just be like God the Creator, but thought he was better than God the Creator and wanted to overthrow God and take his place because Satan believed that he could do things better than God. Satan wanted the glory and praise that was given to God. Satan grew to become lifted up in pride so badly that the Wisdom God gave him was turned into self-glorification and exaltation resulting in a new type of wisdom, the wisdom of himself or Satan.

Over time Satan's evil desires and ambition grew to the point where he was able to deceive a third of the angels or heavenly hosts to rebel against God resulting in them being cast out of heaven down to planet earth. Now let's apply what we know about the nature of Satan while looking at his wisdom. James the brother of Jesus records this insight into the Wisdom of God that comes from above verses earthly wisdom and Satan's wisdom which is described as sensual and devilish.

James 3:13-17, "Who is a wise man and endued with knowledge among you? Let him shew out of a good conversation his works with meekness of wisdom; But if ye have bitter envying and strife in your hearts, glory not, and lie not against the truth; this wisdom descendeth not from above, but is earthly, sensual, devilish; for where envying and strife is, there is confusion and every evil work: but the Wisdom that is from above is first pure, then peaceable, gentle, and easy to be entreated, full of mercy and good fruits, without partiality, and without hypocrisy."

The Book of James is the only place in the Bible containing the three types of wisdoms in the same verse of scripture at the same time. This allows for a precise examination of Satan's wisdom because we can compare it to the qualities found in God's Wisdom. The birthplace of Satan's wisdom was heaven and it came forth out of him. His wisdom is the complete opposite of Godly Wisdom and can be called Anti-Wisdom, just like there is an Anti-Christ. The text begins by showing the signs of Godly Wisdom which comes from above. It portrays a good lifestyle, conversation and ultimately works coming forth as a result of her fruits. A wise person endued with Godly Wisdom can be recognized by a meek and humble spirit, but that doesn't equate to weakness. Following are the signs of both earthly and devilish wisdom which are contrary to Godly Wisdom. The text points out that a person whose heart is filled with Satan's wisdom will produce fruits of bitterness, envy, strife and lies against the truth. His wisdom produces or invents confusion and every evil form of works.

The text ends with a comparison between Godly and Devilish Wisdom. The difference of good and bad fruit produced by two types of trees symbolizes their opposing natures. A person filled with the fruit of the Wisdom from above is honest, peaceable, gentle, easy to be entreated, full of mercy and good works. They are not racists, bigots, sexists or known to have the respect of people because they didn't eat that tree's fruit. Hypocrisy is not their friend but peace and righteousness follows them day and night. Since we have already revealed the fruit of Satan's tree, the only thing to add is the obvious, which is, the fruit of his wisdom is completely opposite of God's.

Furthermore, his wisdom is cunning and full of deceit while being able to transform its appearance into an angel of light resembling God's Wisdom for a short period of time. If the fear of the Lord is the beginning of Godly Wisdom; meaning to be afraid or respect, causing one to be submissive and obedient like children are to their parents. And, if the beginning implies having the controlling principle that directs a person's pathway. Then disbelief and disobedience leads a person into Satan's wisdom.

CHAPTER FIVE:
LADY WISDOM

The word "wisdom" appears 234 times in the Bible, with over half of its usage being found in the book of Proverbs. Proverbs literally means comparison or to compare to. Basically, the book compares the ways of folly to wisdom. Because wisdom is referred to as her and she often in Proverbs; many scholars, teachers, clergy and historians have named wisdom, "Lady Wisdom." For example, chapter one and Verses 20-21 which is the first time we see Lady Wisdom. She is believed to be personified as a prophetess calling out to people in public places.

"Wisdom crieth without, she uttereth her voice in the streets: she crieth in the chief place of concourse, in the openings of the gates, in the city she uttereth her words saying." Verses like this one have been written off as a poetic theme with wisdom depicted as a prophetess or lady character in a scene; however, there can be no disputing the fact wisdom is called a female and by adding what has been revealed in previous chapters the preponderance of evidence leans towards Lady Wisdom being a female spirit.

Historically, there could be more than what meets the eye here. Going back to the days of Moses holding grievances, disputes and lawsuits by the children of Israel from morning till night prompting his father-in-law to intervene with words of wisdom by instructing Moses to pick out Elders of tribes to hold these meetings with Moses handling the cases which couldn't be resolved. Then there is the story of Ruth and Boaz who settled his next of kin case at the gates of the city with the Elders. And one of Jesus' trials was held outside in public because this was common practice.

Therefore, when looking at Verses 20 and 21 in a historical setting, the verse takes on a non-poetic theme. In fact, mothers, families, employees, wives and anyone with disputes took their cases to the city gates seeking justice. Crowds would voice their opinions and demands just like the verses depict. Even in the days we are living in, there are demonstrations that are held in the streets with people crying out for justice and equality. They represent the voices of wisdom seeking fairness in a system that caters to the establishment and the rich and powerful.

There is an interesting play of words which complicates the old way of thinking concerning Lady Wisdom found in chapter two, verses 4 to 8. "If thou seekest her as silver, and searchest for her as for hid treasures; then shalt thou understand the fear of the Lord, and find the knowledge of God; for the Lord giveth wisdom, out of his mouth cometh knowledge and understanding; He layeth up sound wisdom for the righteous, he is a buckler to them that walk upright; He keepeth the paths of judgment, and preserveth the way of his saints."

Overlooked in these verses that is in plain view, but no one wants to talk about or discuss, is that God is referred to as "He" twice without anyone questioning whether this is a poetic character even though it is mentioned in the same verses where wisdom is referred to as "her." And without giving it a second thought, Lady Wisdom is of course recognized as a poetic character. Incredibly, verses 16 through 19, focuses on a type of woman that is immoral and is skilled in seducing men even with her speech. This woman will do anything in order to catch her man while leading him away from the teachings of his parents and forsaking God's laws. Like the story of Samson and Delila, anyone foolish enough to fall for this stranger's charms will end up in sexual sin and blindness. Not able to see where he was and where he now is, or who he was and who he has become.

"To deliver thee from the strange woman, even from the stranger which flattereth with her words; which forsaketh the guide of her youth, and forgetteth the covenant of her God.

For her house inclineth unto death and her paths unto the dead; none that go in unto her return again, neither take they hold of the paths of life. "

Now these verses are filled with the same phrases depicting a lady or woman and use the nouns "she" and "her" just like the verses which define these same pro- nouns as Lady Wisdom being a poetic character. But surprisingly, there is no disputing the fact that in this instance, these nouns and the woman are defined as an actual female or woman.

The question is why? One of the most popular and valued scriptures in the Bible concerning Wisdom is found in the middle of the third chapter, verses 13-21. There is a gold mine of evidence pointing to the prejudice surrounding Lady Wisdom. For instance, my son is used and is often mentioned in Proverbs without question. If "my son" is a poetic character or a parent's actual son. There is no question that the writer is talking about an actual son. But where "she" and "her' is concerned, even being used in the exact same context as "my son", there is a collaborative effort to ignore the connection to Lady Wisdom as a real female spirit. Furthermore, there should be no doubt that the author is referring to Godly Wisdom.

"Happy is the man that findeth wisdom, and the man that getteth understanding; for the merchandise of it is better than the merchandise of silver, and the gain thereof than fine gold; she is more precious than rubies: and all the things thou canst desire are not to be compared unto her; length of days is in her right hand, and in her left-hand riches and honor; her ways are ways of pleasantness, and all her paths are peace; she is a tree of life to them that lay hold upon her: and happy is every man that retained her; The Lord by wisdom hath founded the earth; by understanding hath he established the heavens: by his knowledge the depths are broken up, and the clouds drop down the dew; my son, let not them depart from thine eyes: keep sound wisdom and discretion. "

The writer begins chapter four with a brief insight into whom he is talking to, why he is talking and the purpose behind his communication. He jumps into the the heart of his proverb in the fifth verse:

"Get wisdom, get understanding, forget it not; neither decline from the words of my mouth; forsake her not, and she shall preserve thee, love her, and she shall keep thee; wisdom is the principal thing, therefore get wisdom and with all thy getting, get understanding. Exalt her, and she shall promote thee: she shall bring thee to honor, when thou dost embrace her; she shall give to thine head an ornament of grace: a crown of glory shall she deliver to thee; hear, O my son, and receive my sayings, and the years of thy life shall be many; I have taught thee in the way of wisdom; I have led thee in right paths."

This verse takes on a different style because it is written like a father instructing his son in the form of a personal letter. Solomon makes it clear that he was taught Godly wisdom chiefly by his mother, and his father chimed in from time to time. The writing doesn't show any signs of being poetic in nature; yet Lady Wisdom is still spoken of as "she" and "her." Still scholars, teachers, clergy and historians refuse to give any credence to the idea that Lady Wisdom is a female. There is a deliberate refusal to connect the two together even though other notable religions of the same time period and later recognized female deities:

- Isis – Egyptian
- Allat or Athirat – Arabian
- Belet Nagar – Mesopotamia
- Asherah – Hittites and Canaanites
- Aphrodite – Greek
- Venus – Roman
- Artimus – Greek
- Cerridwen – Irish
- Diana – Roman
- Devi or Shukti
- Kuen Yin
- Lakshml

But deities or goddesses aren't even on the radar in this instance: the focus here is naming a very important spirit that God created as a female person named wisdom. And let's keep in mind that the "ghost of Christmas past" in the movie A Christmas Carol, was a "Female Spirit" and no one gave it any thought. However, for some strange reason, when it comes to the Bible the idea is deemed preposterous. Are we saying then that there are no female angels or beings in heaven? Are we saying there are only male angels or beings and the only female beings are the women that God created on earth?

Certainly, the latter is absolutely ridiculous and based upon nothing but male chauvinistic ideology. Another key theme in these verses center around the fact that Lady Wisdom can be taught and passed down to future generations. Solomon states that he learned Godly Wisdom because his parents took the time to teach him about Wisdom; likewise, Solomon is teaching his son about Lady Wisdom.

Still the most telling aspect of this whole argument seems to be based upon how this scripture was written as compared to other verses viewed as poetic in nature. And, if this verse is not; then, the writer is defining the "father" as King David, the "mother" as Bathsheba or Uriah's wife, "my son" as Solomon, the writer and Wisdom as a female. Obviously, there are a lot of chapters and verses in Proverbs which are appropriately defined as poetic. The problem is men are using this as a basis for dismissing the idea of wisdom being a "her" or "she" which is stated in the text. However, the same standard is not being applied when the text addresses other so-called characters; such as, "the father," "the mother," "my son," and "strange women." For logic's sake, each of these names are treated as they are found in the context in which they appear in the scripture; but not wisdom, whenever "her" and "she" appears in connection to Wisdom an explanation is created to dismiss the relationship as it appears in scripture.

Lady Wisdom is not only found to be personified as a woman in the book of Proverbs but she can be seen and identified as a woman in Judaism with the Torah. The passages of Bar 3:9-4 and 4 portray wisdom as a woman, and Sir 24:23-24 does as well. Then there is the writings called; The Wisdom of Solomon, where we see her as "the spirit of Sophia" and in Wis 7:7-10, she is the breath of God's power. The Talmud and Midrash depict wisdom in the feminine sense or as a woman.

For some reason there is no problem with identifying the church as a bride or woman, in fact, the church is symbolized over 100 times in the Bible as a woman, bride, or virgin. Ephesians 5:25-32 states, "husbands, love your wives, just as Christ also loved the Church and gave Himself for Her." Likewise, Israel is identified or symbolized as a woman or harlot over 150 times in the Bible without anyone questioning the validity of the relationship. Jeremiah the prophet depicts both Israel and Judah in terms of a female. The first appearance in Jeremiah's account can be found in Chapter 3, Verse 8: "And I saw, when for all the causes whereby backsliding Israel committed adultery I had put her away, and given her a bill of divorce, yet her treacherous sister Judah feared not, but went and played the harlot also."

Is The Holy Spirit a He?

Apparently, the use of a woman or female in the Bible as a symbol is alright, but there is a problem when defining or suggesting that a major spiritual entity/person is a female. However, there is no problem or debating the reverse in scripture. Let's look at two of the most recognizable scriptures in the New Testament which parallels the verses relating to Lady Wisdom. There is a striking resemblance between the portrayal and style of the text regardless of their places in the Bible. Uniquely positioned in the Gospel of John are verses relating to the Holy Ghost or Holy Spirit.

John presents The Holy Spirit as "He" in a very similar manner that Solomon defines Wisdom as "her" or "she."

> *John 14:16-26: "And I will pray the Father, and he shall give you another Comforter, that he may abide with you forever; even the Spirit of truth whom the world cannot receive because it seeth him not, neither knoweth him: but ye know him, for he dwelleth with you, and shall be in you; I will not leave you comfortless: I will come to you; but the Comforter, who is the Holy Ghost, whom the Father will send in my name, he shall teach you all things, and bring all things to your remembrance, whatsoever I have said unto you."*

> *John 16:7-14: "Nevertheless I tell you the truth, it is expedient for you that I go away, for if I go not away, the Comforter will not come unto you, but if I depart, I will send him unto you; and when he is come, he will reprove the world of sin, and of righteousness, and of judgment; of sin, because the prince of this world is judged; I have yet many things to say unto you, but ye cannot hear them now; howbeit when he, the Spirit of truth is come, he will guide you into all truth; for he shall not speak of himself, but whatsoever he shall hear, that shall he speak; and he will shew you things to come; he will shew you things to come; he shall glorify me: for he shall receive of mine and shall shew it unto you."*

Positioned in the New Testament with Jesus as the instructor and pinned by John, the Son of Zebedee, also known as the beloved disciple. John's gospel was completed while he was at Ephesus around

A.D. 85. This explains the intimate nature of the above verses. John's perspective is that of a person who had a close relationship with Jesus the Christ and exposes the fact that he walked, talked, ate and slept with the Lord. Like Solomon's writing in Proverbs these verses reflect a letter written in the format and style of a personal letter.

Because of these factors there is no questioning the identity of the Holy Spirit who is referenced as "he" in the above verses. The Holy Spirit, who is the third person in the Trinity, is identified in the Hebrew and Greek text as a male. Furthermore, the pronoun of the word "he" in reference to the Holy Spirit is defined in both the Hebrew and Greek as a male pronoun. So, what if the verses that are found in the Gospel of John depicting the Holy Spirit as "He" were written in the book of Proverbs? Would these two verses be considered as poetic in nature? Clearly, identifying the Holy Spirit as "He" is not up to interpretation because he is the third person in the Trinity. And, what if verses in the book of Proverbs identifying Wisdom as "she" or "her" were found in the New Testament? Logic would dictate that Lady Wisdom would have to be seen as "her" or "she" person or spiritual entity, like the Holy Spirit is seen as "he" or male entity, because she cannot be written off under the cloak of being written as a character in a poetic writing.

What if there exist scriptures in the New Testament that clearly show Lady Wisdom as a "her" or "she" like in Proverbs? Surely all doubt surrounding the validity of the claim would be laid to rest. Well, there exist not just one or two scriptures; but there are three scriptures in the New Testament that no one was thought to either look for; or knew were in the New Testament; but did not want it to be revealed.

Lady Wisdom in the New Testament

Overlooked in the New Testament exist three verses which prove beyond a shadow of a doubt that Godly Wisdom is a female spirit or being. When these verses are tied to what has been uncovered thus far, there is only one conclusion a person can arrive at, which is, the Lady Wisdom depicted in the book of Proverbs is in fact a female. This is huge because wisdom will never be looked at the same again. All that we know about wisdom and have been led to believe about her is based on the premise that wisdom is Jesus, The Holy Spirit or a male angelic being. In fact, there does not exist anywhere in the Bible a female angelic or spirit being of any rank or authority until now. And to be perfectly honest, I can't recall hearing of any angels, beasts, heavenly hosts or spirits associated with a female in the Bible. And what is even more disturbing is that no one has ever questioned why!

It is time to reveal a basic truth concerning Wisdom or Godly Wisdom which has been right in plain sight for all these centuries just waiting to be uncovered. Found in the Gospel of Mark, chapter 6 and verse 2, is the first verse in the New Testament that proves this hidden truth. "And when the sabbath day was come, he began to teach in the synagogue, and many hearing him were astonished, saying: from whence hath this man these things? And what wisdom is this which is given unto him, that even such mighty works are wrought by his hands?"

The word wisdom mentioned in this verse relates to a feminine noun or pronoun in both the Arabic and Roman or Greek languages which means that the wisdom mentioned is in the female tense. In other words, the wisdom referred in this verse is a female version of the word. In fact, this wisdom is directly related to a female entity. There is another aspect of this verse that needs to be looked at which impacts the validity of wisdom and Jesus being two distinctly separate persons. The verse states that the people knew Jesus had been given a wisdom that was far superior to the knowledge and wisdom of the synagogue's rabbis and teachers who were confounded by Jesus.

Also, it was well known that Jesus didn't receive any formal education or training. One thing was known concerning Jesus; no one could deny the miracles he performed nor the wisdom he possessed.

> Luke 7:31-35: "And the Lord said, whereunto then shall I liken the men of this generation? And to what are they like? They are like unto children sitting in the marketplace, and calling one to another, and saying, we have piped unto you, and ye have not danced; we have mourned to you, and ye have not wept; for John the Baptist came neither eating bread nor drinking wine, and ye say, he hath a devil; The Son of Man is come eating and drinking, and ye say, behold a gluttonous man, and a winebibber, a friend of publicans and sinners! But Wisdom is Justified of all "Her" children."

The Gospel of Luke records a stunning statement made by Jesus in the seventh chapter, verses thirty-one through 35 which has a direct impact on the person of Wisdom. There is no doubt that Jesus is speaking because the verses are in red and verse thirty-one begins with Jesus or the "Lord" being identified by the author Luke, as the one speaking. This is huge because of what follows in his speech. For some unknown reason this portion of scripture has been overlooked by biblical historians and scholars, not to mention the clergy and church.

Jesus calls Wisdom "Her"

Jesus does something before deliberately exposing the truth about Lady Wisdom that removes all doubt concerning who is speaking. After dealing with how the religious leaders treated John the Baptist; he turns the focus of the speech to himself with three commonly used words depicting who he is, "The Son of Man."

Twice, the verse mentions that Jesus is the speaker which adds even more credibility to the statements found in the text. There is no debate on who the Son of Man is because it is mentioned numerous times in the New Testament and each time Jesus is calling himself, "The Son of Man", when he is speaking. When following the flow of the text, for some strange reason Jesus turns the attention of the conversation to Lady Wisdom. Hidden in plain sight is this amazing truth defining Wisdom which has been intentionally overlooked because it can't be disputed. Jesus said Wisdom is justified of all "Her" children. Jesus; the Messiah, the Creator, the Son of God and the Son of Man, defines Wisdom as "Her." In other words: wisdom is called her, she or female by the Lord who was in the beginning with God the Father.

This leaves no doubt to the identity and person of whom we call Wisdom. If Jesus says that wisdom is a female or her, then that is who wisdom is. Wisdom is a female spirit, and "Her name is Wisdom."

The Gospel of Matthew records the exact same verse as Luke 7:31-35 and remains one of the few times in the gospels that identical verses are recorded or written by two different authors. Ironically, only the last four verses of each chapter are the same. The verses before these four or which lead into the subject verses are different.

There is no evidence that these two authors ever met because Matthew, who was a tax collector, was Jewish and one of the twelve disciples of Jesus; while Luke, the physician, was Greek and appeared on the scene well after Jesus' resurrection as a disciple of Paul. Furthermore, Matthew's gospel was believed to have been written between 50 and 60 A.D., while Luke was written between 62 and 70 A.D. if not later.

Because the verses are mentioned in two separate Gospels they must be treated and recognized as two different accounts just like the other works and acts of the Four Gospels in the Bible. Each Gospel is looked upon as being inspired by the Holy Spirit and each Gospel is considered as the Word of God. Therefore, this is the second Gospel which records Jesus calling Wisdom "her" or a female, and "Her name is Wisdom."

The evidence is overwhelming, and the case made for the female identification of Wisdom goes without saying. Jesus called wisdom "her" which matches what Proverbs says about wisdom. The Hebrew, Arabic, and Greek or Roman pronouns and nouns for "wisdom" which are feminine solidify her identity as being female. This is not a coincidence but a flag waving in the pages of the Bible for believers.

A very popular phrase says that the proof is in the pudding, and in this case, the proof is in the scriptures contained in the Bible. The person of wisdom is clearly identified by Jesus in two separate gospels as a woman when he addressed wisdom as "her." This is the proof we have been looking for because Jesus did not address wisdom as a he, which contradicts popular beliefs. We are left with a compelling truth; wisdom is justified by her children. And her children need to know who she is. Her name is Wisdom.

ABOUT THE AUTHOR

 Willie Faulkner is a native of Evansville, Indiana. In 1985, he was led by the Spirit to move to Michigan City, Indiana and become a member of Life Temple COGIC. In 1987 he was appointed to the role of a deacon until being called into the ministry two years later. His military unit was activated to the Gulf War in 1990 and upon his return, he became a Sunday School Teacher in 1992. Willie Faulkner, affectionately called "brother Willie," was ordained in 1993 under the jurisdiction of Churches of God In Christ, International.

Currently, Elder Willie Faulkner serves at Life Temple COGIC as a Sunday School Teacher, Bible Class Teacher, Assistant Pastor, and Executive Board Member. Married for 39 years to Rhonda Fleming Faulkner, the couple has been blessed to have 3 children and 4 grandchildren.

After researching biblical, historical, archeological and Jewish writings on the subject of Wisdom; brother Willie, was inspired by the Holy Spirit to share this revelation which proves that Wisdom is a female spirit after finding scriptures where Jesus identifies Wisdom as "her".